Paid to Wait

PAID TO WAIT

Turning Volatility into Cash Flow

A disciplined approach to income-focused investing

Colin Goldsmith

Published by:
Paid to Wait Pty Ltd
ABN 95 695 944 195

Sydney, NSW, Australia

www.paidtowait.com.au

First Edition

ISBN 978-1-7645933-0-4

Cover design and interior layout by Colin Goldsmith.

Who this book is for

This book is written for investors who believe capital should produce income — not simply wait for appreciation.

It is intended for readers who want a structured way to think about portfolio income and the role volatility can play in generating it.

You may find this framework particularly relevant if you are:

An investor seeking reliable income
Many portfolios focus primarily on growth. This book explores how income can become a deliberate objective rather than a by-product of market appreciation.

Approaching retirement or already retired
When income becomes essential, relying solely on capital gains can introduce unnecessary uncertainty. This framework examines how portfolios may generate ongoing cash flow while remaining invested.

An experienced investor looking for structure
If you are already familiar with listed options or income strategies, this book introduces a disciplined framework for organising them within defined risk boundaries.

A financial adviser or portfolio manager
Professionals responsible for managing capital may find the structural principles and income framework useful when considering how portfolios can generate repeatable income.

Markets remain unpredictable. Risk cannot be eliminated.

What this book offers is a structured way to think about capital, income, and volatility — and how those elements can be organised deliberately within listed markets.

Dedication

To my daughter, Carly.

As you pursue your own path as a writer, I hope this book reminds you that disciplined ideas, written clearly, can compound over time.

Love,
Dad

Philosophy

Capital should either work —
or be compensated for waiting.

Framework

Structure provides consistency during uncertainty.

Strategy

Volatility becomes repeatable income.

Preface

The problem facing many investors today is a lack of income.

Living costs continue to rise, and portfolios are not keeping pace.

Investors are told to stay diversified, remain patient, and trust long-term growth.

But growth does not always arrive when income is required.

I question whether the dominant investment approach is aligned with real-world financial pressures.

Many portfolios are built to optimise long-term returns. They are not built to generate deliberate, reliable income.

This book begins from a different starting point:

Income as the objective — not an afterthought.

Paid to Wait outlines a structured way to convert market volatility into cash flow within defined limits.

This is not a trading manual.

It is a way of thinking differently about capital — and the income it produces.

The goal is not to forecast markets, but to structure capital so it is paid for participating in them.

Markets will always fluctuate.
Volatility will always exist.

The question is whether you are paid for it.

Acknowledgements

This book developed over many years of observing markets, managing capital, and working with investors. The ideas within it were shaped not only by study and experience, but also by countless conversations about risk, patience, and discipline.

I am grateful to the clients, colleagues, mentors, and principals whose questions and perspectives helped refine many of the concepts presented here.

I thank my wife and children for the patience they showed during my late-night writing sessions.

During the preparation of this manuscript, artificial intelligence tools, including ChatGPT, were used to assist with editing, structuring ideas, and refining language. All concepts, interpretations, and final editorial decisions remain those of the author.

Financial Disclaimer

This book is provided for general information and educational purposes only. It does not constitute personal financial advice, investment advice, tax advice, legal advice, or a recommendation to engage in any specific strategy, security, or transaction. Nothing in this publication constitutes a financial product recommendation within the meaning of the Corporations Act 2001 (Cth).

The concepts and examples discussed are illustrative only and do not take into account your individual objectives, financial situation, or needs. Before acting on any information contained in this book, you should consider whether it is appropriate to your circumstances and seek independent professional advice where necessary.

All investing involves risk. Capital can be lost. Past performance is not a reliable indicator of future performance. Income objectives discussed in this book are targets, not guarantees. Examples are simplified for clarity and do not reflect actual client outcomes.

The Option Wheel strategy and related concepts involve the use of exchange-traded options and may not be suitable for all investors. These instruments carry risks and require a clear understanding of obligations, margin requirements, liquidity considerations, and potential outcomes.

While reasonable care has been taken in preparing this publication, no responsibility is accepted for errors, omissions, or changes in market conditions after publication.

References to MC Private Wealth Pty Ltd, MoonCunningham Financial Services Pty Ltd, and any associated entities are provided for background and identification purposes only. This publication is not issued on behalf of those entities and does not constitute financial product advice, an offer of services, or a financial product recommendation by them. Reading this book does not create a client relationship, advisory relationship, or fiduciary obligation with the author or any associated entity.

Any opinions expressed are those of the author alone.

Contents

CHAPTER 1

The Income Illusion

Most portfolios are built to look successful.
Few are built to pay the bills.

Imagine an investor with a $1 million portfolio.
On paper, everything looks fine.
The balance has grown over time.
The statements show respectable long-term returns.

But the portfolio produces only $20,000 a year in income.

Living costs are rising.
The investor needs closer to $60,000.

The difference must come from selling assets.
Selling during weak markets.
Selling when prices are unfavourable.
Selling pieces of the portfolio that were meant to provide security.

This is the **income illusion**.

Across much of the developed world, the cost of living has risen sharply.

In Australia, it is felt weekly — not in headlines, but at the checkout.

Groceries cost more.
Electricity and gas cost more.
Insurance costs more.
Almost everything costs more.

What once felt manageable now feels tight.

According to the Australian Bureau of Statistics, headline inflation has remained elevated, sitting above the Reserve Bank's preferred 2–3% target range.

That sustained pressure has shown up in housing, food, insurance and utilities — the everyday expenses people feel most acutely.

But rising costs are only half the story.

The deeper problem is that our income — whether wages, retirement savings, or portfolio returns — often fails to keep pace.

That gap is where pressure builds.

For years, investors have been sold the same story:

Put your money into a diversified portfolio.
Leave it there.
Over time, everything will work out.
Income will come later.
Growth is what matters now.

It sounds sensible.

It just does not work particularly well in the real world.

You cannot pay for groceries with a seven-year investment timeframe.
You cannot pay the electricity bill with unrealised gains.
And you cannot ignore inflation simply because markets are having a difficult year.

This way of thinking comes from something called *Modern Portfolio Theory*.

On paper, Modern Portfolio Theory looks reassuring.
A neat pie chart.
Colourful segments.

Comforting words like diversification, balance, and risk profile.

It promises that if money is spread carefully enough, nothing too bad can happen.

The chart looks calm.
Scientific.
Very grown-up.

But comfort is not the same as certainty.

When markets are stressed, those neat slices tend to move together.
Income disappears.
Volatility feels very real.
And suddenly, the portfolio that looked so sensible no longer feels particularly useful.

You do not need to understand the mathematics to understand the outcome.

In simple terms, Modern Portfolio Theory encourages spreading money across many investments so that risk averages out over time.

The problem is what happens next.

Portfolios become so diversified that no single holding truly matters.
Returns dilute.
Income thins.

After platform fees, fund management costs, advice fees, tax, and inflation, many investors are left treading water

— particularly when measured by the income their portfolio actually produces.

What remains is the hope that capital growth will eventually close the gap.

Hope has never been a reliable strategy.

Excessive diversification does not remove risk.
It often obscures it.

It increases the risk that a portfolio:

Fails to keep pace with inflation.
Produces too little income to matter.
Feels stable on paper but fragile in practice.

In other words, you may feel diversified — and still be going backwards in real terms.

Inflation is the quiet enemy here.

If a portfolio earns 6% after fees while the real cost of living rises by 4%, progress is marginal. Yet within traditional portfolio construction, delivering a modest margin above inflation is often described as success.

If that return comes mostly from capital growth rather than income, the benefit may not even be felt unless assets are sold.

That introduces tax consequences.
Timing risk.
Emotional pressure — usually at the worst possible moment.

The income illusion is believing you are financially secure because your portfolio has grown — even though it does not reliably produce income.

On paper, everything looks fine.

Statements show gains.
Balances rise.
Long-term averages appear respectable.

But growth is not income.
Growth is potential.
Income is usable.
You can only spend cash flow.

When portfolios are built primarily for growth, investors assume that one day they will convert that growth into income.

That assumption depends on three things:

Markets being cooperative.
Timing being favourable.
Capital not being required during weak periods.

If any of those conditions fail, the illusion becomes obvious.

The portfolio may look healthy.

But it does not do the job it was supposed to do.

So let us return to first principles.

Capital should first be preserved before it is deployed.
Structure must precede strategy.
Income must be intentional.

Every investor has a choice.

Capital can sit in cash.
It can sit in term deposits.
It can sit in monetary reserves such as physical gold.

These represent the baseline.
They are not exciting.
They do not require optimism.

Any capital committed beyond that baseline must justify itself.

It must represent immediate or future cash flow — and that cash flow must compensate for risk.

If it does not, there is no reason to move.

Paid to Wait.

Capital should either work — or be compensated for waiting.

Rather than spreading money thinly across dozens of ideas and hoping inflation behaves, I focus on strategies designed to generate income deliberately — month after month — while remaining flexible when conditions change.

A central component of this approach is the use of listed options to structure income deliberately.

One practical implementation of this structure is known as the *Option Wheel strategy*, which we will examine later in the book.

It is not about predicting market direction.

It is about using time, volatility, and clearly defined obligations to generate income from assets I am prepared to own.

Rather than buying and hoping, the structure is built around being paid to enter and being paid to exit.

Income is received upfront.
Outcomes are defined in advance.
Risk is controlled through position sizing and diversification.

The strategy is applied across multiple assets simultaneously.

This creates a portfolio of income streams rather than reliance on a single outcome.

Importantly, this is not passive or mechanical.

It requires experience.
Judgment.
Restraint.

The value is not in the idea itself, but in how it is executed and managed over time.

This book introduces that framework.

It is not about forecasting the future.

It is about building portfolios that continue to function when markets are noisy, inflation is persistent, and living costs keep rising — because that is the world we actually live in.

CHAPTER 2

How Growth Became the Default

And Why It May No Longer Fit

Most investors believe they are building wealth.

Many are simply building balances on paper rather than income they can use.

There is a difference.

Across the investment industry, the dominant message has been consistent:

Buy quality assets.
Stay diversified.
Give it time.
Growth will solve the problem.

But growth does not pay the mortgage.

Income does.

The Accumulation Mindset

Most investment frameworks were designed for the accumulation phase of life.

Earn.
Save.
Invest.
Repeat.

During this phase, income from investments is largely irrelevant. Employment provides cash flow. Market volatility feels temporary. Downturns are uncomfortable but recoverable.

Growth-first portfolios suit this stage well enough.

The problem is that many investors never structurally leave it.

Portfolios are rarely redesigned.
They are simply held longer.

When the Assumptions Change

At some point, the assumptions underlying a growth-first strategy begin to shift.

Living costs rise.
Retirement approaches.
Time horizons shorten.

Suddenly, the portfolio is no longer there to maximise future potential.
It is there to support present reality.

This is where the mismatch appears.

A portfolio designed to grow capital does not automatically transform into one designed to produce income.

Yet investors are often encouraged to behave as though it will.

The Industry's Quiet Incentives

There is another reason growth became the default.

Growth is easier to sell.

It is easier to measure performance against benchmarks than against lived outcomes.

It is easier to charge fees on assets under management than on income delivered.

And it is easier to justify inactivity when the narrative is long-term appreciation.

Income, by contrast, forces accountability.

It must arrive.
It must be usable.
It must endure across conditions.

So when investors reach the point where income matters, the industry response is rarely structural redesign.

Instead, expectations are adjusted.

Unit sales are reframed as "withdrawal strategies."
Volatility is explained away.
Diversification is reinforced.
The underlying portfolio often remains largely unchanged.

Why Retrofits Rarely Work

Converting a growth portfolio into an income solution after the fact is difficult.

Unrealised gains must be sold.
Tax consequences appear.
Market timing becomes critical.

Mistakes become harder to recover from because there is less time and less flexibility.

What once felt like patience now feels like exposure.

This is not because growth is inherently flawed.

It is because growth-first portfolios were never designed to support income.

Growth Still Has a Place

None of this is an argument against growth.

Growth is valuable.

It always will be.

But it is optional.

Income is not.

Every investor eventually reaches a point where capital must contribute to lifestyle rather than simply compound on paper.

The exact timing differs.

The destination does not.

Ignoring that reality does not delay it.

It only makes the transition harder.

Designing With the End in Mind

Choosing income earlier changes the equation.

It introduces intentionality.
It reduces dependence on favourable timing.
It aligns the portfolio with how money is actually used.

This requires a different mindset.
Different tools.
Different assumptions.

It also requires letting go of the idea that complexity automatically produces better outcomes.

The goal is not to chase every opportunity.

It is to build a portfolio that continues to function when conditions are ordinary, uneven, or uncomfortable.

In the next chapter, I will step back and examine the theory that shaped modern portfolio construction — where it came from, what it was designed to solve, and why its assumptions deserve re-examination.

Because understanding how we got here is the first step to choosing a different path.

CHAPTER 3

Modern Portfolio Theory: Origins and Limitations

Modern Portfolio Theory did not begin as a problem. It began as a solution.

When it was developed in the mid-twentieth century, financial markets were structurally different from today.

Markets were simpler.
Products were fewer.
Leverage was modest.
Investors largely accessed securities directly, not through layered platforms and intermediaries.

The central question was straightforward:

How could investors reduce risk without sacrificing expected return?

In 1952, economist Harry Markowitz formalised the answer in his paper *Portfolio Selection*.
The work later earned a Nobel Prize in Economic Sciences in 1990, cementing its influence across academic and institutional investing.

At its core, the theory formalised diversification.

Rather than concentrating capital in a handful of assets, investors were encouraged to combine holdings whose returns did not always move together.
In theory, losses in one area would be offset by gains in another.

Risk, as defined by the model, was volatility.

If volatility could be smoothed through diversification, portfolios could achieve more consistent outcomes over time.

The framework was later visualised through what became known as the "efficient frontier" — a curve representing the highest expected return for each level of volatility. Investors could choose their position along that curve depending on their tolerance for fluctuation.

In the environment it was designed for, this logic was sound.

The Assumptions Beneath the Model

Like all models, Modern Portfolio Theory rests on assumptions.

Some are explicit.
Others are implied.

It assumes that markets are broadly efficient.
It assumes that correlations behave predictably.
It assumes that investors act rationally.
And most importantly, it assumes that time is abundant.

When those assumptions hold, the model functions reasonably well.

The difficulty is what happens when they do not.

When Theory Meets Reality

Over time, the investment landscape changed.

Markets became more interconnected.
Financial products multiplied.
Leverage increased.

Behaviour — fear, greed, and herding — began to dominate outcomes during periods of stress.

In practice, diversification often behaved differently than expected.

When markets were calm, correlations appeared low.
When markets were stressed, correlations rose.
Assets that were assumed to be independent suddenly moved together.

During the 2008 Global Financial Crisis, when panic set in, liquidity evaporated.
Whatever could be sold was sold.

This was not a failure of mathematics.
It was a failure of assumptions.

The Cost of Stagnation

History is less generous than many assume.

The decade from 2000 to 2009 is often referred to as the "lost decade" for equity investors.

The early 2000s began with the technology bubble bursting.
They ended with the Global Financial Crisis.

In between, major global equity markets delivered little real progress once inflation was considered.

Prices moved.
Volatility arrived.
But purchasing power barely advanced.

This was not a collapse.
It was stagnation.

The U.S. S&P 500 experienced multiple years of negative or minimal real performance.
Recoveries occurred.
But progress was uneven.
And time passed.

In Australia, the S&P/ASX 200 also took years to meaningfully exceed prior highs.

Markets did not disappear.
They simply went nowhere for a long time.

And stagnation quietly erodes confidence faster than sharp declines.

Extended periods of modest or stagnant real returns are not anomalies.
They are part of normal market cycles.

Looking forward, many developed economies face structural headwinds.

Ageing populations.
Elevated debt levels.
Persistent inflationary pressures.

None of these guarantee stagnation.

But they do suggest that relying exclusively on capital growth may require more patience than many investors assume.

Stock markets do not rise in straight lines.
They move in cycles.

Sometimes upward.
Sometimes sideways for years.
And sometimes sharply downward.

When time is abundant, those cycles are uncomfortable.

When income is required, they are consequential.

Volatility Is Not the Only Risk

Another limitation of Modern Portfolio Theory is how it defines risk.

By focusing on volatility, the theory treats all price movement as undesirable.

Yet volatility, in itself, does not prevent an investor from meeting obligations.

Running out of income does.
Being forced to sell assets at the wrong time does.
Losing control over capital does.

These risks are lived, not measured.

They matter far more to real people than short-term price fluctuations.

How the Model Was Stretched

As the theory gained acceptance, it began to be used for purposes it was never designed to serve.

Portfolio construction became increasingly standardised.
Model portfolios multiplied.
Allocation decisions were guided more by predefined

frameworks and software outputs than by ongoing human judgment.

Once assets were allocated according to a model, they often remained there indefinitely.

Rebalancing replaced real reassessment.

Portfolios became structured — but less adaptive.

This suited the industry.

Models scale easily.
Processes are repeatable.
Fees are predictable.

But markets are not static.
Nor are investors' needs.

The Cost of Treating Models as Truth

Modern Portfolio Theory was never meant to be a belief system.
It was meant to be a tool.

When tools are treated as truths, flexibility disappears.
Portfolios drift.
Risks become hidden.
Investors are told to trust the process even when outcomes disappoint.

This is how portfolios end up well diversified, professionally managed, and poorly aligned with everyday needs.
The portfolio may satisfy the model, but it may not satisfy the investor.

The theory itself is not a failure.
But it has been extended far beyond its original purpose.

Modern Portfolio Theory was not wrong.
It was simply built for a different financial world.

Why This Matters Now

Today's environment places very different demands on capital.

Inflation is persistent.
Living costs are rising.
And investors are increasingly reliant on their portfolios to contribute to income, rather than simply grow quietly in the background.

A framework built around minimising volatility and smoothing long-term averages struggles to address these realities.

This does not mean Modern Portfolio Theory should be abandoned entirely.
It means its limitations must be acknowledged.

Models can inform decisions.
They should not define them.

In the next chapter, the discussion shifts from theory to structure.
Before discussing returns, forecasts, or optimisation, we must first examine how capital is organised, controlled, and protected.

Without structural clarity, even the most elegant model cannot produce durable outcomes.

CHAPTER 4

Structure Before Strategy

Most investment failures begin long before they are visible.

They begin in structure.

Portfolios are assembled without clarity around control.

Assets are layered inside vehicles that obscure ownership.

Complexity is accepted in place of understanding.

When markets are rising, these weaknesses remain hidden.

When conditions tighten, they are exposed.

Returns fluctuate.

Structure determines survival.

Why Structure Comes First

Investors often focus on performance first.

What will it return?

How much can it grow?

What is the forecast?

But those questions come second.

Before asking what an investment might earn, a more basic question must be answered:

Is the structure sound?

Structure determines:

What is owned.
How it is owned.
Who controls it.

How it can be exited.
Where the true risks sit.

If structure is weak, optimisation is irrelevant.

If structure is fragile, valuation cannot save it.

Hidden Fragility

Many portfolios appear diversified, balanced, and professionally managed.

But structure is rarely examined closely.

Ownership may be indirect.

Liquidity may depend on others.

Decision-making authority may sit far from the investor.

Under normal conditions, this feels efficient.

Under stress, the cracks show.

Structure, not theory, determines resilience.

Survival Before Optimisation

Models attempt to optimise risk and return.

Structure determines whether capital survives long enough for optimisation to matter.

Survival precedes performance.

Control precedes return.

Clarity precedes growth.

Without structural integrity, performance becomes accidental.

A Different Starting Point

For this reason, my framework begins with structure.

Not forecasts.

Not predictions.

Not asset allocation models.

Structure defines what is investable.

Only after structure is sound does the question of return become relevant.

Only then does capital need to justify its deployment.

In the next chapter, I will outline the five structural principles that guide every portfolio decision.

They are not complex.

They are not theoretical.

They are practical constraints designed to protect capital before it is ever put at risk.

CHAPTER 5

Five Structural Principles

If structure determines survival, then structure must come first.

And it must be intentional.

Before considering expected returns, forecasts, or valuation models, I apply five structural principles.

Applied consistently, they provide a layer of protection for everything built on top of them.

1. Direct Ownership

I prioritise assets that are owned directly and transparently.

If I cannot clearly identify what is owned, who controls it, and how it can be exited, it does not belong in the portfolio.

Control matters.

Indirect structures often function smoothly in stable conditions.

Under stress, they reveal who truly has authority — and it is rarely the investor.

Direct ownership reduces structural fragility.

It preserves clarity.

It limits dependency on intermediaries.

And it ensures capital remains under deliberate control.

2. Tangible Assets

I focus on assets with real economic substance.

Operating businesses.
Productive companies.
Cash.
Physical gold and selected precious metals.

These assets exist independently of financial engineering.

Their prices fluctuate.

Their substance does not.

Tangible assets anchor portfolios in reality.

They reduce reliance on narratives.

They increase reliance on fundamentals.

3. Enhanced Income

Income is not incidental.
It is intentional.

The portfolio is designed to generate meaningful, repeatable cash flow as a primary goal — not as an afterthought to capital growth.

Enhanced income serves three purposes.

It funds lifestyle without forced sales.
It reduces dependence on favourable market timing.
And it accelerates capital efficiency by returning cash to the investor regularly.

Without income, investors must eventually sell assets to live.
With income, capital can remain invested while still producing results.

This is not yield chasing.
It is yield engineering.

Income is generated within defined limits.
Exposure is controlled.
Risk is measured.

The aim is not maximum income.
It is sustainable income.

Structured.
Repeatable.
Deliberate.

4. Tax Efficient

Returns only matter after tax.

The structure of an investment influences the character and timing of income.

Ignoring tax at the design stage creates friction later.

This principle does not require aggressive strategies.

It requires awareness.

Capital should move efficiently.

5. Agile in Execution

Markets change.

Conditions evolve.

Rigid structures struggle in dynamic environments.

I favour approaches that allow exposure to be adjusted, risk to be managed, and capital to be repositioned when necessary.

Agility does not mean constant activity.

Often, restraint is the most disciplined action.

It preserves the ability to respond when conditions demand it.

Structure Before Valuation

Together, these five principles form a structural filter.

They protect against:

Loss of control.
Hidden fragility.
Forced decisions.
Permanent capital impairment.

Only after this structure is sound does valuation become relevant.

Only then does capital need to justify its deployment through risk-free benchmarks and intrinsic value assessment.

Structure protects capital.

Valuation determines when and where to deploy it.

In the next chapter, I will explain how capital is committed within this framework — and why limiting exposure is often more important than selecting the perfect asset.

Because how much you risk often matters more than what you risk it on.

CHAPTER 6

When Capital Deserves to Be Deployed

Structure protects capital.

The next question is simple:

When does capital deserve to be deployed?

Not every opportunity justifies risk.
Not every idea deserves funding.

Before committing capital, two filters must be applied.

The First Benchmark: The Risk-free Return

Every investment decision begins with a basic question:

Why take risk at all?

Capital always has alternatives.

It can remain in cash.
It can sit in term deposits.
Or it can be held in physical gold — a monetary reserve that does not depend on anyone else's promise.

This is the baseline.
Capital that does not require risk to justify itself.
It may not be exciting.
But it exists.

If an investment cannot reasonably be expected to outperform that baseline — after adjusting for risk — then it does not deserve capital.

The benchmark is not a stock index.
It is not peer performance.
It is what capital can earn by doing very little.

Risk must be compensated.
Otherwise, it is unnecessary.

The Second Benchmark: Intrinsic Value

The second question is just as important:

What is this asset actually worth?

Price is what the market says today.
Value is what the business is likely to produce over time.

Strip everything else away and an asset is only worth the cash it can generate in the future.

Not the story.
Not the theme.
Not the recent price movement.

Future net cash flow.

For operating businesses, that cash flow comes from earnings.
Earnings that can be retained, reinvested, or distributed.

Intrinsic value is simply the present value of those future earnings — adjusted for risk.

That is it.

The underlying asset does not need to pay income directly to me.
I have other methods for generating cash flow.

But if I am prepared to own the business, it must stand on its own economic foundation.

If there is no identifiable stream of value beneath the price, there is no intrinsic value.

There is only speculation.

When price is reasonable relative to value, ownership is justified.

And when ownership is justified, structuring income around that ownership becomes logical — not hopeful.

The Risk of Doing Too Much

Many investment mistakes do not begin with bad assets.

They begin with good ideas taken too far.

Too much capital.
Too quickly.
With no flexibility if conditions change.

Being fully invested sounds efficient.

In practice, it can be fragile.

When all capital is committed, every market movement feels amplified.
Small changes feel large.
Temporary setbacks feel permanent.

And the only response is to sell.

Usually at the wrong time.

Volatility becomes loss — not because markets fell, but because flexibility was absent.

Position Size Is Risk

Even strong investments can produce poor outcomes if they are sized incorrectly.

A position that feels manageable at 10% may feel intolerable at 30%.

The asset has not changed.
The exposure has.

This is why restraint matters more than conviction.

Conviction feels productive.
Restraint protects longevity.

Capital preserved is opportunity preserved.

Capital Commitment Within an Income Framework

An income-focused structure removes the need to be fully invested.

Income can be generated without committing all capital at once.
There is no need to rush.

Targets can be met without stretching.

Activity adjusts to pricing and opportunity — not emotion.

Instead of asking:

"How much can I put to work?"

The better question becomes:

"How much is required to achieve the objective?"

Once that objective is met, there is no requirement to push further.

Excess risk rarely improves outcomes.
It often shortens time horizons.

Discipline Before Opportunity

Markets are rarely ideal.

They pause.
They stall.
They move sideways.
They fall.

Capital deployed without discipline amplifies these movements.

Capital deployed deliberately can absorb them.

The risk-free baseline prevents unnecessary risk.
Intrinsic value justifies ownership.
Position sizing preserves flexibility.

Together, they ensure capital moves with intent — not urgency.

In the next chapter, we will examine the environment where this discipline matters most: extended periods where prices make little progress.

These environments expose growth-first portfolios.

They reward patience.

Particularly when patience is compensated.

CHAPTER 7

The Market That Breaks Most Portfolios

When people think about market risk, they imagine extremes.

Booms.
Crashes.
Headlines.

What they rarely consider is the market that does very little at all.

Sideways markets do not feel dramatic.
They do not create panic.
They rarely create euphoria.

They simply persist.

And over time, they quietly inflict damage.

The Market No One Plans For

Sideways markets are periods where prices fluctuate but make little meaningful progress.

Years can pass.

Portfolios move.

Statements look active.

But purchasing power barely advances.

For growth-focused investors, this environment is corrosive.

There is no momentum to lean on.

No rising tide to smooth errors.

No visible reward for patience.

Time, instead of helping, begins to undermine confidence.

Why Growth Struggles Here

Growth strategies rely on appreciation.

When prices stall, that appreciation fails to arrive.

Returns become uneven.

Recoveries feel slow and incomplete.

Inflation erodes purchasing power quietly in the background.

On paper, nothing appears broken.

In reality, progress has stalled.

This is where the income illusion becomes visible.

A portfolio may appear stable.
But without cash flow, the investor remains suspended — waiting for an outcome that may not arrive on schedule.

Inflation's Quiet Pressure

Sideways markets are especially damaging when inflation persists.

Even modest inflation continues working against capital each year.

While asset prices drift, the cost of living advances steadily.

The portfolio may not decline.

But it may still fall behind.

This gap rarely announces itself.

It emerges gradually — through reduced flexibility, rising anxiety, and an increasing reliance on favourable future conditions.

Why Income Changes the Experience

Income strategies behave differently in sideways markets.

They do not depend on rising prices to function.

Cash flow continues even when valuations stagnate.

Time becomes productive rather than punitive.

This does not eliminate risk.

Assets still fluctuate.

Volatility remains.

But the portfolio is doing something useful while waiting.

That distinction matters.

Behaviour Is the Real Variable

Sideways markets are not only a test of strategy.

They are a test of behaviour.

Investors relying solely on growth often become restless.

They second-guess decisions.

They chase new narratives.

Or they abandon strategy in search of movement.

Income provides an anchor.

Regular cash flow reduces the urge to act unnecessarily.

It reassures the investor that the portfolio is still functioning — even when markets appear indifferent.

This behavioural advantage builds quietly over time.

The Most Common Outcome

History shows that multi-year periods of flat or muted real returns are not rare.
They are recurring features of equity markets.

They rarely dominate headlines.

But they dominate lived experience.

Designing portfolios for rising markets is easy.

Designing them for stagnation requires a system.

And most investors never build one.

Why This Environment Matters

Sideways markets expose the weakness of growth-first portfolios without spectacle.

There is no crash to blame.

No dramatic turning point.

Just time passing.

Income-first portfolios reveal their advantage most clearly here.

They generate cash flow.

They preserve flexibility.

They reduce reliance on hope.

In the next chapter, I will begin to show how income can be generated deliberately — not through prediction, but through structure — using tools that work with time rather than against it.

Because the market that appears to do nothing often determines who compounds — and who merely waits.

And it is precisely the market most investors never plan for.

CHAPTER 8

What Income Really Means

Before going further, **income** needs to be defined clearly.

Not as a marketing term.
Not as a yield printed on a factsheet.
Not as a projected return.

Income is cash received.

Usable.
Repeatable.
Not dependent on selling the asset.

In this framework, income is money received while ownership remains intact.

If capital must be sold to generate cash, that is not income.

It is liquidation.

Liquidation reduces the base of income producing assets. Income does not.

Liquidation converts ownership into spending power. Income preserves ownership while generating spending power.

That difference is structural.

And structure determines outcomes.

Income Comes From Obligation

True income arises because an obligation exists.

A dividend declared from profits.

Interest paid for the use of capital.

Or a premium received in exchange for accepting defined terms.

Income is not hope.

It is compensation.

It is contractual.

And it arrives independent of market direction.

Paid to Wait

Being paid to wait arises from defined obligations — formal agreements with clear terms.

Those agreements specify:

The price you are willing to buy.
The price you are willing to sell.
The expiry of that obligation.
And the compensation received for making that commitment.

Income is received first.
The outcome follows later.

That sequence changes behaviour.

It reduces urgency.
It removes dependence on growth arriving on schedule.

In this framework, the primary source of income is premium from exchange-traded options.

That is deliberate.

The terms are standardised.
The premium is paid upfront.
And it does not require prices to rise in order to exist.

Compensation comes from commitment — not prediction.

That is what it means to be paid to wait.

What Income Is — and Is Not

Dividends are welcome.
But they are not the engine.
They depend on company profits and board decisions.

Interest earned on reserved capital is helpful.
But it is secondary.

Capital gains are beneficial.
But they are not income.
They depend on market movement.

Income does not require markets to rise.
It requires structure.

This is not an argument against dividends.
Or rental income from property.
Or interest from lending.

It is an argument for precision.

In this book, income refers primarily to option premium generated on listed securities through exchange-traded contracts.

Everything else is additional.

The aim is simple:

Income first.
Outcomes follow.

In the next chapter, we move from philosophy to mechanism — and examine how Paid to Wait operates in practice.

CHAPTER 9

Turning Volatility into Cash Flow

Most investors fear volatility.

When prices swing sharply, confidence drops.
Headlines grow louder.
Commentators grow urgent.
Statements grow uncomfortable.

Volatility is treated as the enemy.

But volatility is not the enemy.

Uncompensated volatility is.

The Misunderstood Force

Volatility reflects uncertainty.

Prices adjust.
Expectations shift.
Risk is repriced in real time.

That movement feels threatening when returns depend solely on price appreciation.

When prices fall, growth disappears.

But volatility has another characteristic.

It has value.

When uncertainty rises, defined outcomes become more valuable.
Protection costs more.
Flexibility costs more.
Time itself carries a price.

That repricing creates opportunity.

Pricing Uncertainty

Option premium expands as volatility rises.

Premium is not arbitrary.
It reflects participants transferring risk at a price.

Hedgers seek protection.
Speculators seek leverage.
Institutions adjust exposure.
Market makers facilitate liquidity.

The result is the same:

Uncertainty is priced.

Premium is compensation for accepting defined obligations within that risk.

Most investors experience volatility passively.
They endure it.
They hope it fades.

Paid to Wait approaches it differently.

It does not avoid volatility.
It engages with it.

Income is received upfront in exchange for commitment.

Risk remains.
But it is priced.

Uncertainty is no longer endured.
It is compensated.

In this sense, the approach is a form of compensated investing.

Rather than simply waiting for markets to rise, investors structure their capital so that waiting itself produces income.

Movement Is Enough

Traditional strategies require markets to rise.

Paid to Wait requires markets to move.

Movement creates repricing.
Repricing creates premium.

Volatility does not need to be predicted.
It only needs to exist.

Markets will fluctuate.
Economic cycles will repeat.
Uncertainty will persist.

The difference lies in the response.

Treat volatility as a threat.
Or treat it as a source of compensation.

The Paid to Wait philosophy is simple:

If markets are going to move anyway, they may as well pay you.

But philosophy alone is not enough.

Turning volatility into cash flow requires structure.
It requires a defined mechanism.

That mechanism has a name.

The Option Wheel.

CHAPTER 10

The Engine Behind Paid to Wait

Investing is often described as the art of buying well and selling well.
Paid to Wait simply adds a third idea: being compensated while waiting to do both.

It is an investment philosophy that reframes volatility as something that can be priced rather than feared.
It challenges the assumption that portfolios must depend primarily on appreciation.

But philosophy alone does not generate income.
For that, a mechanism is required.

That mechanism is the **Option Wheel strategy** — or simply, the Option Wheel.

What the Engine Actually Does

The Option Wheel converts time and volatility into income.

It operates through exchange-traded options on listed securities.

Not forecasts.
Not predictions.
Contracts.

Contracts to buy a quality asset at a defined price.
Contracts to sell an owned asset at a defined price.

In each case, compensation is received upfront for accepting that obligation.

Premium is paid first.
The outcome is determined later.

That order matters.

Income precedes resolution.

The True Drivers: Time and Volatility

Two forces power the engine:

Volatility.
And time.

Volatility determines how much uncertainty is priced into a contract.
Greater uncertainty generally increases premium.

Time determines how long that uncertainty exists.

Every option contract has a finite life.
As expiry approaches, time value decays.

This decay is continuous.

The Option Wheel does not resist these forces.
It works with them.

Volatility expands pricing.
Time compresses value.

Both contribute to income generation.

Markets do not need to rise.
They need to fluctuate.

And time must pass.

The Core Components

At its simplest, the Option Wheel operates through two distinct legs:

Being paid to wait to buy.
Being paid to wait to sell.

These are implemented using:

Cash-secured puts.
Covered calls.

Nothing exotic.
No hidden leverage.
No complex structures.

Defined commitment.
Defined pricing.
Defined compensation.

Why It Is Called a Wheel

The process is cyclical.

If a put expires unexercised, premium is retained and capital remains available.
If shares are assigned, ownership begins.
While owned, covered calls may generate additional income.
If shares are called away, capital is released.

Then the process begins again.

Compensated entry.
Income during ownership.

Compensated exit.
Repeat.

That repetition is the wheel.

Engine — Not Shortcut

The Option Wheel is simple in design.

It is not simplistic in execution.

Asset selection matters.
Position sizing matters.
Capital allocation matters.
Risk mitigation parameters matter.

This is not speculation.

It is structured income generation built on listed contracts and economic value.

Paid to Wait is the philosophy.

The Option Wheel is the engine that makes it operational.

In the next chapter, we examine the first component:

Being paid to wait to buy.

If you are willing to purchase a company at a particular price, it is rational to require compensation while waiting for that price to arrive.

CHAPTER 11

Being Paid to Wait to Buy

Most investors buy first.

Then they wait.

They wait for growth.
They wait for dividends.
They wait for the market to confirm the decision.

Paid to Wait reverses the sequence.

It waits first.
And it is compensated for waiting.

Buying With Compensation

Writing a cash-secured put creates an obligation.

An obligation to buy a quality asset at a defined price, on or before a defined date.

In exchange for accepting that obligation, premium is received upfront.

That premium is the income.

If the market never declines to the agreed price, the premium is retained and capital remains available.

If the market declines and the shares are assigned, ownership begins — and the premium is still retained.

Either outcome is defined in advance.

Price is defined.
Time is defined.
Compensation is defined.

Nothing is left to impulse.

Why This Matters

Traditional investors often say:

"I will buy if it comes down."

But they are not compensated while waiting.

Time passes.
Capital sits idle.
Intention has no price.

The cash-secured put formalises that intention.

It converts a desired entry price into a listed contract.

Waiting becomes structured.
Structure becomes income.

A Different Starting Point

Instead of asking:

"What should I buy today?"

The better question becomes:

"At what price would I be willing to own this business?"

That price becomes the strike.

The premium becomes the compensation for patience.

If the strike is never reached, income is retained and capital remains flexible.

If the strike is reached, ownership begins at a price that was selected deliberately — and compensated.

There is no chasing.
No reactive entry.
No dependence on short-term forecasts.

Structure Over Forecasting

This approach does not require predicting direction.

It does not require calling market bottoms.

It requires selecting suitable assets.
Defining acceptable terms.
And accepting compensation for commitment.

The outcome may vary.

The structure does not.

The First Rotation of the Wheel

If shares are not assigned, the process can be repeated.

If shares are assigned, the next phase begins:

Being paid to wait to sell.

That is the second leg of the engine.

And that is where the wheel completes its first full rotation.

CHAPTER 12

Being Paid to Wait to Sell

Ownership does not end the process.

For many investors, buying is the decision.
After that, they wait.
They hope the price rises.
They hope dividends grow.
They hope time works in their favour.

Ownership is not the end of the structure. It is the next phase of it.

Holding With Compensation

A covered call is an agreement to sell an asset already owned at a defined price.

In exchange for accepting that obligation, premium is received upfront.

The commitment is clear.
The price and expiry date are defined.
The premium arrives first.

If the asset never reaches the agreed sale price, ownership remains — and the premium is retained.

If it does reach that price, the asset is sold — and the premium is still retained.

Either outcome is acceptable. Compensation is received in both cases.

Turning Ownership into Income

Ownership can be passive.

Or it can be structured.

A covered call converts time into income.

It transforms dormant capital into productive capital.

Instead of relying solely on appreciation, the structure receives payment for defining an exit level in advance.

The asset price may rise, fall, or move sideways.

Regardless of direction, time is passing.

And time decay works continuously through the life of the contract.

Defined Outcomes

The contract formalises an intention that already exists.

If the asset reaches the agreed sale price before or at expiry, it is sold.
Capital is released.
The premium is retained.

If it does not, ownership continues.
The premium is retained.
And the process can repeat.

Both outcomes were acceptable from the outset.

The Option Wheel – the basic process

Now the wheel becomes visible.

Be paid to wait to buy.
Be paid to wait to sell.

Each leg is compensated.
Each action is deliberate.
Each contract reduces reliance on prediction.

This is not about chasing maximum upside.

It is about defining acceptable outcomes — and being paid while they resolve.

From Position to Portfolio

When both legs are applied thoughtfully, capital efficiency improves.

Income accumulates without requiring perfect timing.

Markets may rise.
They may stall.
They may fall.

Premium is received upfront.
Time passes.
Contracts expire.
And the process can begin again.

Applied to a single asset, this structure is effective.

Applied across multiple assets, it becomes more powerful.

Because one wheel generates income.
Many wheels generate regular cash flow.

CHAPTER 13

Many Wheels Are a System

A single wheel on a single asset can generate income.

But one wheel alone does not produce regular and reliable cash flow.

It is a position.

The strength appears when the structure is applied across multiple suitable assets at the same time.

Not concentrated.
Not random.
Deliberate.

Diversification With Purpose

Traditional diversification spreads capital across multiple assets and waits for growth.

Paid to Wait spreads defined agreements across selected assets and receives compensation across all.

Each asset has:

Defined entry levels.
Defined exit levels.
Defined capital allocation.

Income is not dependent on one outcome.

It is distributed.

If one asset is assigned into ownership, others may expire unexercised.
If one is called away, others continue generating premium.

The portfolio breathes.

Staggered Exposure

Option contracts do not need to share identical timeframes.

Some expire sooner.
Some later.
Some are written into the next cycle.

This reduces concentration around any single expiry date or market event.

Time becomes layered.
Income becomes steadier.

Capital Allocation Matters

Not all wheels deserve equal capital.

Some assets justify larger allocation.
Others require restraint.

Volatility differs.
Premium differs.
Business quality differs.

Capital follows those realities.

The aim is not maximum activity.

It is balanced income generation within defined limits.

System Over Signal

Operating multiple wheels changes the mindset.

This is no longer about whether one asset rises or falls.

It becomes the management of a portfolio of contracts.

Some expire unexercised.
Some are assigned into ownership.
Some are assigned into sale.

Across the portfolio, premium accumulates.

Not perfectly.
Not evenly.
But consistently.

Philosophy at Scale

When applied across multiple assets, the Paid to Wait approach becomes visible at scale.

Capital rotates.
Exposure shifts.
Contracts cycle.

The Option Wheel functions as a portfolio engine.
The philosophy provides the discipline that guides it.

In the next chapter, we examine how total capital commitment is measured and limited within this structure.

Because scale increases opportunity.
It also increases exposure.
And exposure must be controlled.

CHAPTER 14

Capital Commitment & Exposure Control

Income generation is only meaningful if capital survives.

Before discussing targets or percentages, one question must be answered:

How much capital is actually at risk?

This is where otherwise sensible approaches become vulnerable.

Not because the idea is flawed.

But because exposure quietly expands.

Total Commitment Pool vs Current Commitment

In this structure, a clear distinction exists between the total commitment pool and capital currently engaged.

The total commitment pool represents the maximum capital allocated to support potential assignment.

It does not mean all of that capital is deployed at once.

At any given time:

Some capital is actively committed to existing agreements.

Some portion of the commitment pool remains unutilised — held in cash or long stock positions awaiting deployment.

Separate from this, there may also be an additional buffer of accumulated cash or shares outside the commitment pool.

And depending on broader financial circumstances, a further allocation may be held as a portfolio reserve — often in gold, selected precious metals, or term deposits.

Clarity here prevents overreach.

A cash-secured put requires cash to be set aside.

A covered call requires shares already owned.

No leverage.

No scrambling for capital after the fact.

And no requirement to deploy everything at once.

All activity operates within defined risk mitigation parameters.

Full Deployment Reduces Flexibility

Being fully invested can appear efficient.

It often reduces flexibility.

When every dollar within the commitment pool is engaged, there is no room to adjust.

No room to respond.

No room to take advantage of improved pricing.

Volatility then becomes stress rather than opportunity.

Income structures only work when restraint exceeds excitement.

Position Size Is Risk

Risk is not only about direction.

It is about size.

A position that feels manageable at 5% may feel intolerable at 20%.

The asset may be sound.

The exposure may not be.

This is why capital is allocated deliberately across multiple wheels.

No single asset dominates the portfolio.

No single expiry cycle determines outcomes.

Income is distributed.

Exposure is layered.

Measuring Total Exposure

When multiple wheels operate simultaneously, total capital commitment must be measured deliberately.

What percentage of the commitment pool is currently engaged?
What percentage remains unutilised?
What portion of the overall portfolio sits outside the strategy entirely — in buffer or reserve?

These questions are not theoretical.

They are reviewed continuously.

Because income is attractive.

Overexposure is expensive.

Visibility Before Control

Income structures only remain disciplined when exposure is visible.

Every open contract must be tracked.

Not approximately.
Not mentally.
Precisely.

At any point in time, it should be clear:

- How many contracts are open.
- Which assets they relate to.
- The strike prices and expiry dates.
- The capital required to support assignment.
- The total percentage of the commitment pool currently engaged.

If this cannot be seen clearly, it cannot be controlled.

Options create defined obligations.
Defined obligations create defined exposure.
But when multiple wheels operate simultaneously, exposure can expand quietly unless it is measured deliberately.

Expiry clustering must be visible.
Asset concentration must be visible.
Total capital at risk must be visible.

This is not administrative detail.
It is structural discipline.

Without accurate tracking, small increases in exposure accumulate unnoticed.
Confidence grows.
Limits stretch.
Flexibility shrinks.

The framework does not fail suddenly.
It drifts.

Tracking prevents drift.

It ensures that capital commitment remains aligned with predefined limits — not with optimism.

Visibility precedes control.
Control preserves longevity.

Discipline Before Targets

It is tempting to ask:

"How much income can this generate?"

The better question is:

"How much capital should be committed to generate income responsibly?"

Income is meaningless if the capital behind it is overstretched.

Capital preservation comes first.

Income follows.

In the next chapter, we will examine how income is measured against committed capital — and how a defined premium objective is applied within those limits.

Because a target without boundaries is not discipline.
It is risk.

CHAPTER 15

The 1% Objective

Once capital commitment is determined, income can be targeted properly.

Not against total portfolio value.
Not against hope.
But against the committed capital pool.

That shift clarifies everything.

Measuring What Actually Works

If capital is reserved to support defined option contracts, income should be measured against that reserved pool.

Premium is not compared to the entire portfolio.

It is compared to the capital deliberately set aside to produce it.

That removes distortion.

It prevents inflated expectations.

And it forces honesty.

A Disciplined Standard

Within this framework, the objective is straightforward:

To generate approximately 1% per month in option premium — net of trading costs — on committed capital.

Month by month.

Within constraints.

This is not rigid.

There will be months when pricing is thin.

There will be periods where restraint is required.

The objective guides behaviour.

It does not override judgment.

What 1% Looks Like in Practice

Let's make it concrete.

If $100,000 is committed to the pool, a 1% target equates to $1,000 in option premium per month.

If $500,000 is committed, it equates to $5,000.

If $1,000,000 is committed, it equates to $10,000.

Again, this is not measured against total wealth.
It is measured against capital deliberately allocated to generate income.

The calculation is simple.
Consistency is the challenge.

The 1% objective refers specifically to option premium generated on committed capital.

It does not refer to total portfolio return.

It does not imply that share prices will rise.

And it does not prevent capital values from declining when markets fall.

The income component can be controlled.

The market component cannot.

If equity markets decline materially, the value of shares held under this framework will decline as well.

Assignments may increase ownership.

Portfolio valuations will fluctuate.

Premium received softens that impact.

It does not eliminate it.

This distinction matters.

The objective is to generate approximately 1% per month in premium income on committed capital.

It is not a promise of 1% positive total return in every month.

Income can be consistent.

Market prices cannot.

Understanding that separation prevents unrealistic expectations — and the poor decisions that follow them.

The goal is not to stretch beyond limits to hit a number.

It is to structure capital so that contracts generate income consistently — within defined risk mitigation parameters.

Income scales with committed capital.

Exposure remains contained.

That reframes the real question.

Not:

"How much do I need to retire?"

But:

"How much committed capital do I need to produce the income I require?"

That is a structural shift.

Why 1% Matters

At first glance, 1% per month may not seem dramatic.

On an annualised basis, it approximates 12%.

When earned on defined capital — within limits — it becomes meaningful.

Especially when:

Premium is received upfront.
Dividends may be collected while shares are held.
Interest may be earned on cash acting as security.

Income layers.

Quietly.

The objective is consistency.

Not excitement.

Putting 1% in Context

Long-term equity markets have often delivered average nominal returns in the range of 8–10% per annum.

But averages conceal reality.

Returns arrive unevenly.

They cluster.

They stall.

They reverse.

A disciplined 1% monthly income objective — measured against committed capital — equates to roughly 12% per annum before compounding.

The comparison is not about superiority.

It is about timing.

One approach depends on appreciation.

The other depends on defined contracts and priced movement.

Growth requires markets to rise.

Income requires markets to move.

Process Over Yield

Achieving consistent portfolio income does not require every position to produce income every month.

In practice, positions cycle through different stages of the Wheel over time, allowing the portfolio as a whole to generate steady cash flow.

This is not yield chasing.

It is not extracting maximum premium regardless of risk.

The 1% objective reflects structure, experience, and consistent application.

Not aggression.

Not optimism.

Premium levels fluctuate.

Volatility expands in some sectors and contracts in others.

When pricing is elevated, fewer contracts may be required.

When pricing compresses, additional contracts may be written — within limits.

Activity adjusts.

Risk does not.

Structure governs both.

The target never overrides capital control.

All activity operates within defined risk mitigation parameters.

What This Is — And What It Is Not

It is an objective built on:

Selling option contracts.
Established listed markets.
Transparent pricing.
Measured capital commitment.

It is not a guarantee.

Markets shift.

Volatility changes.

Judgment remains essential.

The 1% income objective is a guide.

Not a promise.

The 1% objective is pursued through disciplined capital allocation and structured option writing within defined limits.

While the framework is deliberate, results remain influenced by prevailing market conditions and execution.

Income First

When measured properly, 1% per month on committed capital changes perspective.

Growth becomes secondary.

Income becomes primary.
Capital gains become additional.

The portfolio is no longer waiting for appreciation.
It is receiving compensation for participation.
That reduces pressure.
It replaces hope with structure.

But premium income rarely exists in isolation.
Capital moves through different states within the structure.
And each state can contribute to income in different ways.

In the next chapter, we examine how these income sources combine — and how they form a layered income framework.

CHAPTER 16

Income Layers

Income rarely arrives from a single source.
It should not need to.

Within this framework, premium is primary.
Everything else is secondary.

Capital sits in different states at different times.
Some is committed to contracts.
Some is tied to owned shares.
Some is waiting.

Each state can produce income.

When organised deliberately, income is layered — without increasing exposure.

The Primary Layer: Premium

Option Wheel premium income is the engine.

It is deliberate.
It is contractual.
It is received upfront.

Defined obligations are accepted at defined prices for defined periods.
Compensation arrives first.
Resolution follows later.

The 1% objective refers specifically to this layer — premium measured against committed capital.

This is the focus.

Markets may rise.
Markets may fall.
Premium is structured.

Everything else is additional.

The Secondary Layer: Dividends

When shares are assigned, ownership begins.

While ownership continues, those shares may produce dividends.

Dividends are not engineered.
They depend on earnings and board decisions.

But they are real.

In some cases, dividend timing and yield are considered when structuring positions.
Owning quality businesses through reporting periods can be intentional — not accidental.

Still, dividends are not the focus.

They are participation in the underlying business while the option structure operates around it.

Premium comes first.
Dividends may accompany it.

The Structural Layer: Interest

When a cash-secured put is written, the required capital is set aside.

It is not deployed into the market.
It is held as security for the obligation.

That cash remains in the account.

And it earns interest.

Not because it is being optimised.
Not because yield is being chased.
But because it is there.

Capital reserved for potential assignment is still capital.

It does not sit idle.

While premium is received for accepting the obligation, interest is earned on the cash supporting it.

Two forms of compensation.
One for commitment.
One for time.

In addition, any capital within the commitment pool that is not currently tied to open contracts or share positions also remains in cash and earns interest.

Simple. Structural. Appropriate.

Capital should either work — or be paid while it waits.

How the Layers Coexist

At any point in time:

Some capital supports open contracts.
Some capital is tied to owned shares.
Some capital remains uncommitted.

Premium is generated from written contracts.
Dividends may be received from ownership.
Interest accrues on capital deliberately preserved.

These streams do not compete.

They coexist.

Premium remains the target.
Dividends and interest are additive — not substitutes.

If dividend income is strong in a period, that is welcome.

If interest accumulates while capital waits, that is appropriate.

But the premium objective does not relax because other income exists.

The engine remains the engine.

Organisation — Not Escalation

Layering income is not increasing risk.

There is no borrowing to enhance yield.
No stacking of exposure.
No stretching beyond predefined limits.

Premium is generated only on allocated capital.
Dividends arise from businesses selected deliberately.
Interest accrues on capital intentionally preserved.

This is capital organised properly.

Not capital pushed harder.

A Layered Outcome — With a Single Objective

Premium remains the primary driver.

Dividends may supplement it.
Interest may reinforce it.

But the objective does not change.

Income is structured.
Capital is controlled.
Exposure is measured.

Layering does not dilute discipline.
It supports it.

In the next chapter, we move from layered income to something more tactical — how entry and exit pricing can be structured deliberately, not hopefully.

Because being paid to wait matters.

But where you enter — and where you exit — matters just as much.

CHAPTER 17

Entries & Exits

(Discounts & Markups)

Option Wheel premium is the engine.

But price still matters.

This framework does not ignore capital gains.
It refuses to depend on them.

Instead of chasing appreciation, it structures entry and exit deliberately.

Entry at a Discount

When writing a cash-secured put, the first question is not:

"What will the price do?"

It is:

"At what price would I be willing to own this business?"

That price is selected before the contract is written.

If the market declines to that level, ownership begins.

But ownership does not begin at the prevailing market price.

It begins at a defined price.

Often below where the asset was trading when the contract was written.

And premium has already been received.

That premium reduces the effective entry cost.

This is not buying strength.

It is being compensated to wait for weakness.

If the price never reaches the strike, premium is retained.

If it does, ownership begins at a pre-selected level — adjusted by income already received.

That is deliberate entry.

Not reactive buying.

Defined Exit Levels

The same discipline applies on the way out.

When writing covered calls, the strike price represents a predefined exit.

If the asset reaches that level, it is sold.

Not because of emotion.
Not because of headlines.
Because it was agreed in advance.

Premium is received for making that commitment.

If the price rises beyond the strike, some upside is surrendered.

That is accepted from the outset.

If the strike is not reached, ownership continues — and premium is retained.

Capital is not held indefinitely waiting for a "perfect" price.

Exit levels are structured.

Capital Gains — Targeted, Not Chased

When shares are assigned below prevailing prices and later called away at higher strikes, capital gains occur.

But they are not speculative.

They arise from defined price ranges.

Discounted entry.
A mark-up on exit.

The spread between those levels represents structured appreciation — not open-ended hope.

Sometimes markets rally sharply and exceed the strike.

Sometimes prices drift and contracts expire.

Sometimes ownership persists through multiple cycles.

None of these outcomes requires prediction.

They require structure.

The aim is not to capture every rally.

It is to operate within acceptable ranges — repeatedly.

There will be occasions when markets do not cooperate.

Prices may decline materially.
A defined exit at a mark-up may not be available within acceptable limits.

In those circumstances, capital preservation takes precedence over symmetry.

A deliberate loss is preferable to expanding exposure in pursuit of a recovery that may never arrive.

This is where exposure control matters.

Position sizing and commitment limits exist precisely for these periods — so that an adverse outcome remains contained rather than compounding.

Judgement includes knowing when not to wait.

Tactical — Within Limits

This framework is not passive.

Strike selection matters.
Expiry selection matters.
Position size matters.

Dividend timing may be considered.
Valuation ranges are assessed.
Market conditions are observed.

But activity always operates within predefined risk parameters.

There is no stretching to catch momentum.

No abandoning structure because markets appear enthusiastic.

Precision replaces urgency.

Why This Requires the Right Environment

Defined entry and exit pricing only work when:

Prices are visible.
Contracts are standardised.

Liquidity is real.
Obligations are enforceable.

Without those conditions, structure degrades.

Private agreements introduce ambiguity.
Illiquid vehicles distort pricing.
Intermediaries dilute control.

For entry and exit to remain deliberate, the market itself must be durable.

That is why environment matters.

In the next chapter, we examine why operating within established listed markets is not a preference — it is a requirement.

Because precision depends on transparency.

And structure depends on enforceability.

CHAPTER 18

Why Listed Markets Matter

Income is attractive.

Structure determines whether it lasts.

Once a measurable objective is introduced, the next question becomes unavoidable:
Where does this activity actually take place?

Not all income strategies operate in the same environment.

Some rely on pooled vehicles — managed funds, investment schemes, trust structures — where capital is combined and control is indirect.

Some rely on counterparties whose strength you are simply expected to assume.

This framework does not.

Listed Securities. Listed Options.

All activity takes place on established public stock exchanges.

The shares are listed.
The options are exchange-traded.
Pricing is transparent.
Contracts are standardised.

There are no private side agreements.
No bespoke documentation.
No hidden variations between participants.

Every contract is cleared through a central clearing house.

That is not a minor detail.

It is foundational.

Clearing Houses and Counterparty Risk

When an option is written on an exchange, the clearing house becomes the counterparty.

Not an individual trader.
Not a hedge fund.
Not a single institution.

The clearing house stands between buyer and seller.

Its role is simple: ensure obligations are met.

Positions are marked to market daily within the clearing system.
Margin requirements are recalculated daily.
Capital must be posted.

If obligations cannot be met, the clearing house steps in.

In Australia, ASX Clear (a subsidiary of the Australian Securities Exchange) performs this role.

Globally, central clearing houses operate at scale, processing vast volumes of exchange-traded contracts each day under strict regulatory supervision.

They are heavily regulated, capitalised, and specifically designed to reduce counterparty risk within the financial system.

This does not eliminate market risk.

But it removes reliance on personal trust or private promises.

The contract is backed by the exchange's clearing system — not by the goodwill of the other party.

That matters.

When Structure Fails

Investment problems do not always begin with falling markets.

Sometimes they begin with structure.

Over the past two decades, investors globally have experienced:

Fund suspensions.
Redemption freezes.
Gated withdrawals.
Delayed access to capital.

In many cases, the underlying assets were not worthless.

They were simply illiquid.

Too many investors wanted their money at the same time.

And the structure could not accommodate it.

When liquidity promised exceeds liquidity available, pressure builds quickly.

Complex structures amplify that pressure.

This framework avoids those vulnerabilities by operating in listed markets where:
Prices are visible.
Liquidity is observable.
And obligations are centrally cleared.

Market risk remains.

Access risk is reduced.

No Pooled Structures

Capital is not placed into a pooled vehicle.

It is not subject to redemption gates.

It is not exposed to the behaviour of other investors.

It is not dependent on the liquidity profile of an underlying fund.

Positions are owned directly through an authorised stockbroker.

Control remains with the investor.

This reflects the structural principle of Direct Ownership.

Transparency as Risk Management

Every position has:

A visible strike price.
A visible expiry date.
A visible premium received.

There are no embedded layers of hidden leverage.

No external manager operating outside the framework.

Transparency is not cosmetic.
It is how risk becomes measurable.

Complexity tends to conceal risk.
Clarity exposes it.

The Industry Reality

Long-running industry scorecards tell a consistent story.

Over extended periods — 10 to 20 years — the majority of actively managed equity funds fail to outperform their benchmark after fees.

Many funds disappear.
Some merge.
Few deliver sustained outperformance.

This does not mean skill does not exist.

It means persistent outperformance is rare.

And every additional structural layer increases cost and dependency.

Eliminating Unnecessary Layers

Over time, the investment industry has added layer upon layer:

Platforms.
Funds.
Sub-funds.
Managers.
Advisers.
Administrators.

Each layer takes a fee.

The consequences of layered financial structures are not hypothetical.

Australia's Hayne Royal Commission into Misconduct in the Banking, Superannuation and Financial Services Industry uncovered widespread cases of *"fees for no service,"* where investors were charged ongoing advice fees despite receiving no advice at all.

The inquiry also exposed how vertically integrated institutions — combining product manufacturing, platforms and advice — could create systems where layers of fees accumulate between investors and the assets they ultimately own.

Every additional intermediary between an investor and their capital introduces cost, complexity and distance from the underlying asset.

When too many parties must be paid before the investor benefits, returns are diluted.

Structure becomes heavy.

Accountability becomes blurred.

This framework strips those layers back.

It operates directly within established listed markets.

Capital remains identifiable.
Control remains clear.

Durability Before Scale

Durable means functioning through stress — not just through favourable conditions.

Income objectives are only meaningful if the structure supporting them can withstand pressure.

Exchange-traded markets provide:

Standardisation.
Liquidity.
Regulatory oversight.
Central clearing.

That foundation allows the framework to operate without relying on private agreements or complex pooled vehicles.

Income may fluctuate.
Markets may move.
But the structural framework remains intact.

In the next chapter, we examine the central trade-off that makes this structure possible.

Because income received today is real.
And every dollar of income requires giving up something else.

CHAPTER 19

A Bird in the Hand

Income in this framework is not accidental.
It is chosen.

And choosing income requires a deliberate trade-off.

Options allow investors to exchange open-ended possibility for defined compensation.
Upside becomes limited.
Income becomes certain.

That exchange sits at the centre of the structure.

Choosing Income Over Possibility

When writing options, something deliberate happens.
You exchange open-ended potential for defined compensation.
You accept that if an asset rises sharply, you may sell it earlier than you otherwise would — and at a lower price.
You accept that you will not capture every dollar of appreciation.

In return, you receive income today.

That exchange is not a flaw.
It is the design.

A Bird in the Hand

There is an old saying:
A bird in the hand is worth two in the bush.

In investing terms, the meaning is straightforward.
Certain income today may be more valuable than uncertain gains tomorrow.

When a covered call is written, some upside is surrendered.
When premium is received, future possibility is exchanged for present compensation.

The second bird is left where it is.

The first is secured.

Why Make That Trade-Off?

Because large capital gains are uncertain.

They depend on:

Market sentiment.
Timing.
Company announcements.
Macro conditions.

Premium received today does not.

It is contractual.
It is defined.
It is already earned.

Growth may arrive later.
Income has already arrived.

Discipline Over Optimism

This framework does not chase maximum upside.

It accepts moderated upside in exchange for repeatable income.

That moderation is not a weakness.

It is structural.

And it protects capital.

The aim is not to capture every rally.

It is to build a system that continues to function when markets rise, when they stall, and when they move sharply in either direction.

Because income received today reduces dependence on what tomorrow might bring.

A portfolio should be structured to perform, not to hope.

The Real Advantage

Once income becomes primary, behaviour changes.

You are no longer waiting for price appreciation to justify your strategy.

You are being compensated for participation.

That changes psychology.

It reduces impatience.

It increases restraint.

And over time, that behavioural edge compounds just as powerfully as the income itself.

In the next chapter, we examine why time itself works in favour of this structure — and how time decay quietly rewards the patient option writer.

Because when compensation is received upfront, even waiting becomes productive.

And capital that earns while it waits is capital working as intended.

CHAPTER 20

When Time Works for You

Most investors experience time as something they endure.

They wait for recovery.
They wait for growth.
They wait for markets to cooperate.

Time feels passive.

Sometimes frustrating.

In this framework, time has a role.

Time works.

The Value of Waiting

When an option is sold, premium is received upfront.

Part of that premium reflects uncertainty about the future.

As time passes, that uncertainty reduces.

Even if the underlying asset does nothing, the option gradually loses value.

That erosion is known as time decay.

For the buyer of an option, time is a cost.

For the seller, time is working in the background.

When Nothing Happens

This matters most in quiet markets.

When prices rise sharply, growth investors are satisfied.
When prices fall sharply, risk becomes obvious.

But when markets move sideways, many portfolios stall.

Time passes.
Returns feel flat.

In an option-writing framework, sideways movement is not wasted time.

Premium has already been received.

As expiry approaches, the value of the contract declines.

If the defined price is not reached, the contract expires.

If it is reached, the outcome was pre-agreed.

Either way, the passage of time was not idle.

It was working.

Defined Horizons

Every contract has an expiry date.

Every position has a defined end point.

There is no indefinite holding pattern.

No open-ended "wait and hope."

There is a timeline.

There is a review.

There is a decision.

That alone changes behaviour.

Patience With Terms

Most investors are asked to be patient.

Few are compensated for it.

Here, patience has terms.

You are paid for accepting defined obligations over a defined period.

You are paid for being willing to act at defined prices.

There is no need to predict short-term direction.

There is no urgency to react to every headline.

The clock is moving — whether markets move or not.

Time as an Advantage

Time decay does not remove risk.

Prices can still move sharply.

Assignments can still occur.

But time is no longer neutral.

It gradually reduces the value of sold contracts.

That movement works in favour of the seller.

Markets fluctuate.

The clock moves in one direction.

In the next chapter, we will examine when restraint is required — and why sometimes the correct decision is to do less.

Because time helps.

But judgment determines when to use it.

CHAPTER 21

When Not to Act

Structure sets boundaries.
Time provides advantage.
Neither replaces decision-making.

The most important moves in this framework are often the ones not made.

Not Every Premium Is Attractive

Just because an option can be sold does not mean it should be.

Premium may look high.
High relative to what?

Volatility.
Business quality.
Liquidity.
Balance sheet strength.
Broader conditions.

On the other side, premium may simply be too thin to justify the obligation being taken on.

Premium without context is noise.
Context determines whether it is worth acting.

Quality Still Matters

This framework does not turn weak assets into strong ones.

Selling options on fragile businesses does not reduce fragility.
It concentrates it.

Asset selection remains foundational.

Established listed companies.
Transparent financials.
Sustainable earnings.
Real liquidity.

Income cannot compensate for structural weakness in the underlying asset.

If the foundation is poor, the structure built on top of it will be unstable.

When Conditions Shift

There are periods when volatility compresses broadly.

Premium shrinks.
Pricing thins.

This is not a signal to force activity.
Nor is it automatically a signal to retreat.

It is a signal to reassess.

If premium per contract is lower, more agreements might technically reach the income objective — but only within defined limits.

Alternatively, capital can rotate toward assets where pricing is more rational.

Activity may adjust.
Limits do not.

Operating within parameters is not rigidity.
It is control.

Assignment Is Not Failure

Assignments are outcomes, not mistakes.

If capital has been allocated deliberately, assignment simply transitions the position.

The relevant question is not:
"How do I avoid this?"

It is:
"Was this price acceptable at the start?"

If the answer is yes, the process continues without drama.

Working Within Boundaries

Risk mitigation parameters define maximum exposure.

They do not dictate full utilisation.

They set the ceiling.
They do not demand you reach it.

Conditions may justify operating below the maximum.
Often they should.

Structure defines the outer edge.
You decide how close to that edge you operate.

The Value of Inaction

Sometimes the best decision is no decision.

Premium may not justify risk.
Volatility may not fully price uncertainty.
Liquidity may be insufficient.

Doing nothing is not inactivity.
It is capital preservation.

Capital preserved is flexibility preserved.

Longevity Over Motion

This framework is not built on constant movement.

It is built on repeatable decision-making.

Markets change.
Business cycles rotate.
Pricing expands and contracts.

The objective is not to trade more.
It is to endure longer.

In the next chapter, we examine why this approach is not set-and-forget — and what ongoing management actually requires.

Because structure creates opportunity.
Oversight protects it.

CHAPTER 22

Why This Is Not Set and Forget

Structure provides clarity.
Time provides advantage.
Income provides consistency.

But none of it runs unattended.

This is not a set-and-forget strategy.
It is a managed framework.

Monitoring Is Continuous

Positions are monitored.

Volatility shifts.
Corporate events arise.
Liquidity changes.
Pricing adjusts.

Even when no action is taken, oversight remains active.

You will not see this on a portfolio report.
But it is constant.

Expiry Is a Decision Point

Every agreement has an expiry date.

That date is not administrative.
It is a review point.

Options may expire unexercised.
They may be assigned.
They may be rewritten into the next cycle.

Each outcome requires consideration.

Capital is redeployed deliberately.
Nothing rolls automatically.
Nothing is ignored.

Assignment Is Managed, Not Feared

When shares are assigned, they are reassessed.

Is the position appropriately sized?
Does the underlying still meet quality criteria?
Is further premium writing justified?

Assignment is not a mistake.

But nor is it an excuse for complacency.

Adjustments Are Structural — Not Emotional

Markets do not move in straight lines.

They expand.
They contract.
Volatility rises.
Volatility falls.

This framework does not chase those movements.

Adjustments occur for structural reasons:

When contracts expire.
When assignments occur.
When capital is released.
When allocation limits are approached.
When concentration exceeds predefined boundaries.

Changes are driven by predefined limits — not headlines.

If volatility expands, premium may increase.
If volatility contracts, premium may shrink.

That influences position sizing and exposure.
It does not change the rules.

Capital is reallocated deliberately.
Contracts are written within limits.
Exposure is reviewed before it is increased — not after.

This is not reactive management.
It is structured deployment.

Oversight Preserves the Edge

Time decay provides an advantage.
Premium provides income.
Structure provides boundaries.

But oversight preserves longevity.

Without active monitoring, even a sound framework drifts.
Without review, defined parameters can gradually stretch.

This is why experience matters.
And why judgment cannot be automated.

Process Over Automation

There is a difference between systematic and automatic.

This framework is systematic.
It is not automatic.

Rules guide behaviour.
They do not replace thinking.

The focus is repeatability.
Not rigidity.

Survival is the true measure of success.

But survival only matters if risk is understood honestly.

And market risk never disappears.

CHAPTER 23

Market Risk Remains

Paid to Wait is not a hedge against broad market declines.

It is not designed to eliminate equity risk.

It is designed to define how you are compensated for assuming it.

If stock markets fall sharply and remain depressed, capital values under this strategy will decline as well.

Assignments will occur.
Ownership may increase.
Premium received will soften the impact — but it will not prevent it.

This framework operates inside listed equity markets.

When markets enter sustained bear cycles, the portfolio participates.

Income continues to be generated.
But capital recovery may take time.

This is not a capital preservation strategy.

It is a structured income framework operating inside public equity markets.

The purpose is not to avoid volatility.

It is to be paid for accepting it within defined limits.

During Prolonged Downturns

In extended declines, patience matters.

Capital commitment must remain measured.
Exposure must stay within predefined boundaries.

Activity may adjust.
Restraint becomes even more important.

Premium does not eliminate downturns, but it reduces reliance on perfect timing.

It reduces the pressure to sell into panic.
It provides compensation while markets reprice.

But it does not create immunity.

In severe bear markets, preserving capital may require reducing activity or realising losses. This framework does not remove the need for judgment.

Expectations Determine Behaviour

Unrealistic expectations lead to emotional decisions.

Clear expectations support composure.

Paid to Wait does not promise protection.

It promises a repeatable framework.

And that framework, applied consistently, is what allows capital to remain engaged through difficult conditions without abandoning the process entirely.

Market risk cannot be eliminated.
It can only be defined and priced.

What determines survival, however, is rarely the market alone.
It is how the investor responds to it.

CHAPTER 24

Behaviour Is the Edge

Markets do not defeat investors with mathematics.

They defeat them through behaviour.

Most investment models assume rational actors.
They assume patience during stagnation.
They assume discipline during decline.
They assume restraint when confidence rises.

Experience suggests otherwise.

Markets test temperament before they reward intelligence.

The Silent Variable

Every portfolio contains a variable that cannot be modelled:

The person operating it.

Two investors can hold identical positions.
One remains composed.
The other intervenes at the worst possible moment.

The difference is rarely information.

It is tolerance.

Fear compresses time.
Confidence stretches exposure.
Boredom creates activity.
Regret distorts memory.

Behaviour, not volatility, is what damages most outcomes.

Why Growth Alone Is Difficult to Hold

Growth-first portfolios ask investors to wait.

Wait for recovery.
Wait for appreciation.
Wait for averages to reassert themselves.

While waiting, nothing arrives.

No reinforcement.
No cash flow.
Only price movement.

If prices rise, conviction feels justified.
If prices stall for years, doubt builds.
If prices fall sharply, conviction disappears.

Without income, the experience feels unproductive.

Unproductive capital invites interference.

Interference, mistimed, is expensive.

Income Changes the Experience

Income alters the psychology of waiting.

When premium is received upfront, the portfolio is no longer idle.
It is producing.

Even when markets move sideways, time is working.
Contracts decay.
Cash accumulates.

Capital values may fluctuate.
Assignments may occur.

Risk remains.

But reinforcement exists.

Reinforcement reduces urgency.
Reduced urgency supports discipline.
Discipline protects capital.

Defined Boundaries Prevent Drift

Ambiguity encourages excess.

Without defined limits, exposure expands quietly.
Confidence builds.
Activity increases.

Boundaries exist to prevent this.

A defined monthly objective, measured against committed capital, introduces structure.

If the objective is met, there is no structural reason to stretch.
If pricing is insufficient, there is no need to force activity.

Clarity removes pressure.

Pressure is what causes overreach.

Measured Expansion

There is another behavioural advantage embedded in this framework.

Income, when retained, increases the capital base.

If $1,000,000 is allocated to the commitment pool and income is reinvested rather than withdrawn, that pool may gradually increase.

The percentage objective does not change.

It remains approximately 1% per month.

But 1% of a larger base produces greater income.

Capacity expands — not because exposure has been forced, but because capital has increased through earned income.

That distinction is critical.

Exposure is not increased by reaching further.
It increases because earned income has been redeployed within the same boundaries.

Growth-first strategies depend on rising prices to expand scale.

This framework allows scale to expand through earned income.

Capital increases first.
Then income increases proportionately.

The structure remains constant.

Only the base changes.

Restraint Before Brilliance

Most investment damage occurs during periods of confidence.

Returns arrive.
Exposure drifts upward.
Position sizes expand beyond intention.

When reversal comes, fragility is exposed.

Measured income generation tempers that impulse.

It rewards repetition over aggression.
Sustainability over intensity.

The aim is not intensity.
It is continuity.

Continuity allows the structure to work as designed.

Break continuity — and even sound frameworks fail.

The Real Edge

There is nothing secret here.

The contracts are listed.
The exchanges are transparent.
The rules are public.

The difference lies in operating within limits when it would be easier not to.

In accepting moderated upside.
In leaving capital uncommitted when pricing is insufficient.
In allowing scale to increase gradually through earned income rather than expanding risk abruptly.

Markets will fluctuate.

Volatility will persist.

Structure defines boundaries.
Income provides reinforcement.
Behaviour determines whether those boundaries are respected.

Consistency, sustained across cycles, is what allows capital not only to endure — but to expand deliberately.

CHAPTER 25

Longevity Over Excitement

In markets, excitement is easy to find.

Headlines are loud.
Predictions are constant.
New products appear each cycle promising better returns and faster growth.

Longevity is quieter.

It does not rely on forecasts.
It does not depend on being right about the future.
It depends on durability.

The Real Objective

The purpose of this framework is not to maximise returns in a single year.

It is to generate repeatable income while preserving capital.

Across rising markets.
Across sideways markets.
Across declining markets.

Income first.
Structure governs.
Moderation endures.

Moderation Is Strength

This approach accepts trade-offs.

It surrenders some upside.
It accepts defined boundaries.
It values income received over potential gains imagined.

That moderation is not weakness.

It is intention.

The investor who survives each cycle retains optionality.

The investor who overreaches eventually withdraws.

Durability creates the conditions for results to accumulate.

Alignment Over Optimisation

Modern portfolio construction seeks optimisation.

This framework seeks alignment.

Alignment between:

Income and lifestyle.
Capital commitment and tolerance.
Structure and time horizon.

When income becomes primary, behaviour steadies.

When behaviour steadies, outcomes stabilise.

Confidence follows structure — not prediction.

Returning to the Beginning

This book began with a simple observation:

Living costs rise.
Markets fluctuate.
Income does not automatically keep pace.

The income illusion assumes growth will eventually close that gap.

This framework does not assume.

It structures.

By defining capital commitment, operating within durable public markets, and prioritising income over speculation, the goal shifts.

The portfolio is no longer waiting for relief.

It is working deliberately — whether markets cooperate or not.

Not through prediction.
Not through hope.
But through defined, compensated participation.

Paid to Wait

Capital should either work — or be compensated for waiting.

Notes and Sources

Chapter 1 — Inflation Data

Australian Bureau of Statistics (ABS). *Consumer Price Index, Australia – December 2025.*

Reserve Bank of Australia (RBA). *Statement on Monetary Policy and Inflation Targeting Framework.*

Chapter 3 — Modern Portfolio Theory, Market Stagnation & Long-Term Returns

Markowitz, H. (1952). *Portfolio Selection.* The Journal of Finance, 7(1), 77–91.

Sharpe, W. F. (1964). Capital Asset Prices: A Theory of Market Equilibrium under Conditions of Risk. *The Journal of Finance*, 19(3), 425–442.

Malkiel, B. G. (1973). *A Random Walk Down Wall Street.* W. W. Norton & Company.

Nobel Prize Committee. (1990). The Sveriges Riksbank Prize in Economic Sciences in Memory of Alfred Nobel awarded to Harry Markowitz, Merton Miller and William Sharpe.

S&P Dow Jones Indices. *S&P 500 Annual Returns (Historical Data).*

Market Index. *S&P/ASX 200 Historical Performance Data.*

Dimson, E., Marsh, P., & Staunton, M. *Global Investment Returns Yearbook*. Credit Suisse / UBS (annual publication).

Vanguard Research. *The Case for Low-Cost Investing*. Vanguard Group.

Chapter 3 — Lost Decade Context

Morningstar Australia.
"Unconventional Wisdom: Are We on the Cusp of a Lost Decade?"

Chapter 15 — Long-Term Equity Return Context

Dimson, E., Marsh, P., & Staunton, M. *Global Investment Returns Yearbook*. Credit Suisse / UBS Investment Bank (annual publication).

S&P Dow Jones Indices. *SPIVA Global Scorecard*.

Chapter 16 — Clearing Houses and Central Counterparties

Australian Securities Exchange (ASX).
ASX Clear – Clearing and Settlement Overview.
Explains the role of ASX Clear as the central counterparty for exchange-traded derivatives in Australia.

Bank for International Settlements (BIS).
Statistics on Derivatives and Central Clearing Activity.
Global data on exchange-traded and centrally cleared derivatives volumes.

Reserve Bank of Australia (RBA).
Central Counterparties and Financial Stability (Financial

Stability Review).
Discussion of the role of clearing houses in mitigating counterparty risk.

Chapter 16 — Fund Suspensions & Access Risk

Bank for International Settlements (BIS).
Open-Ended Funds and Liquidity Risk. BIS Quarterly Review.
Discussion of liquidity pressures in pooled investment vehicles.

Financial Stability Board (FSB).
Non-Bank Financial Intermediation and Structural Vulnerabilities Reports.

Reserve Bank of Australia (RBA).
Financial Stability Review (Various Editions).
Discussion of redemption pressures and liquidity stress in managed funds.

Chapter 16 — Active Manager Underperformance

S&P Dow Jones Indices.
SPIVA U.S. Scorecard – Active vs Passive Performance.

S&P Dow Jones Indices.
SPIVA Australia Scorecard.

Chapter 18 — Eliminating Unnecessary Layers

Royal Commission into Misconduct in the Banking, Superannuation and Financial Services Industry. Final Report. Commonwealth of Australia, 2019.

Notes on Sources

Data and research referenced are drawn from publicly available institutional publications and long-running industry scorecards. They are provided for context and illustration only and should not be interpreted as investment recommendations.

Intellectual Influences

No investment framework develops in isolation. The ideas presented in this book were shaped by years of observation, practice, and study, as well as by the work of thoughtful investors and writers who have contributed to the broader discussion of capital allocation and risk.

In particular, the author acknowledges the influence of Roger Montgomery's work on intrinsic value and Return on Equity analysis, most notably presented in *Value.able*. The emphasis on evaluating businesses through their ability to generate strong returns on equity has informed elements of the analytical thinking discussed in this book. A disciplined focus on business quality and capital efficiency provides an important foundation when selecting assets suitable for long-term ownership and income generation.

More broadly, the philosophy of focusing on risk, patience, and rational decision-making owes much to the long tradition of value investing and the writings of investors who emphasise discipline over prediction.

While these influences helped shape the thinking presented here, the framework described in this book reflects the author's own interpretation and application of these ideas.

Any interpretations, applications, or conclusions presented here remain entirely the author's own.

About the Author

Colin Goldsmith is an Australian wealth manager and the creator of the *Paid to Wait* investment framework.

Through his firm, MC Private Wealth, he works with investors seeking disciplined, income-focused strategies designed to generate repeatable cash flow while managing risk.

Colin is a Responsible Manager and Authorised Representative of MoonCunningham Financial Services Pty Ltd (AFSL No. 555843), an Australian Financial Services Licence holder.

He holds a Bachelor of Commerce from the University of Newcastle (Australia) and is a Fellow Chartered Financial Practitioner (FChFP).

Paid to Wait reflects an approach developed through managing capital across multiple market cycles, with an emphasis on structure, transparency, and control.

Colin lives in Central West NSW with his wife Sarah and their three children on a small farm where they raise goats, sheep, and chickens. When not working with clients or writing, he is learning to fly.

The Option Wheel

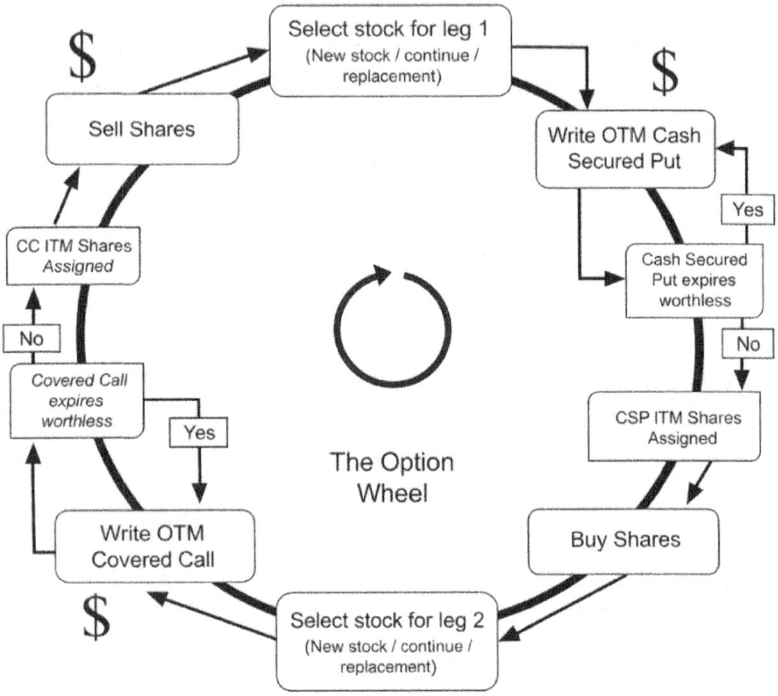

Learn more at

paidtowait.com.au

Coming Next

Paid to Wait

Building the Framework

Paid to Wait explained why.

The next book will explain how.

Execution.

Risk control.

Capital structure.

Capital rotation.

Time decay.

Because structure creates durability.

Precision creates longevity.

Reader Notes

Made in the USA
Monee, IL
04 November 2026

67383009R00098